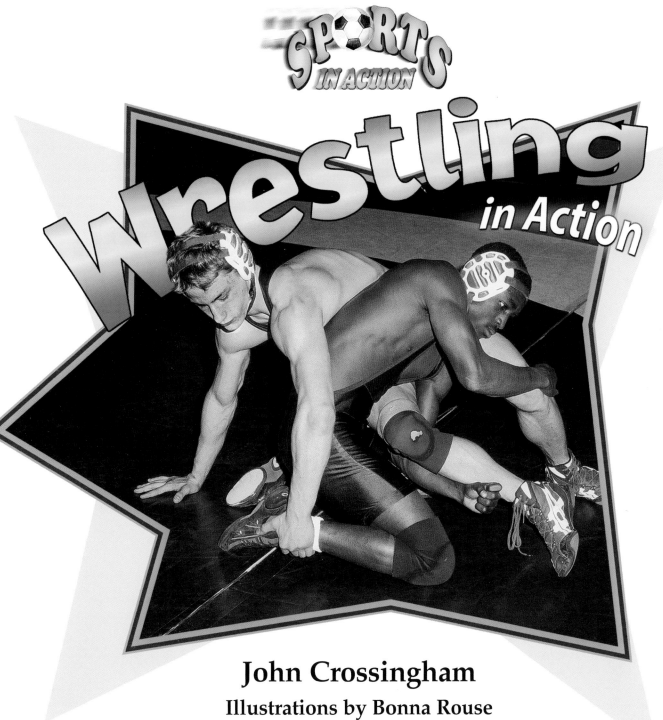

Wrestling
in Action

John Crossingham

Illustrations by Bonna Rouse

Photographs by Marc Crabtree

🜲 Crabtree Publishing Company

www.crabtreebooks.com

Created by Bobbie Kalman

Dedicated by Laura Hysert
To my rasslin' niece Vanessa, whose love always amazes me

Editor-in-Chief
Bobbie Kalman

Author
John Crossingham

Editorial director
Niki Walker

Project editors
Laura Hysert
Rebecca Sjonger

Editor
Kathryn Smithyman

Art director
Robert MacGregor

Design
Margaret Amy Reiach

Production coordinator
Heather Fitzpatrick

Photo research
Laura Hysert

Special thanks to
Josiah Boyd; Sheldon Francis; Attila Kasap; Howard Leung; Ellen Macro; Rebecca Marshall; Victoria McGoldrick; Courtnay Lafond; Katie Mercer; Frank Mensah; Jamie Macari; Nick Cipriano, McMaster University; Tim MaGarrey, Ontario Amateur Wrestling Association; Richard DesChatelets, Brock University; Eric Knuutila, Niagara County Community College

Consultants
Steve Fraser, US National Wrestling Coach, USA Wrestling
Chris Stefopulos, Ontario Amateur Wrestling Association and
  Team Impact Wrestling Club

Photographs
All photographs by Marc Crabtree

Illustrations
All illustrations by Bonna Rouse except:

Museum of Fine Arts, Budapest, Hungary/Bridgeman Art Library:
  page 5

Crabtree Publishing Company

www.crabtreebooks.com   1-800-387-7650

PMB 59051	616 Welland Avenue	Maritime House
350 Fifth Avenue	St. Catharines	Basin Road North,
59th Floor	ON, Canada	Hove
New York, NY	L2M 5V6	BN41 1WR
10118		

Cataloging-in-Publication Data
Crossingham, John
  Wrestling in action / John Crossingham;
illustrations by Bonna Rouse; photographs by Marc Crabtree.
    p. cm. -- (Sports in action)
Includes index.
Offers a brief introduction to the history, techniques, equipment, and rules of wrestling, a sport that began thousands of years ago and was part of the first Olympic games.
  ISBN 0-7787-0356-8 (pbk.) -- ISBN 0-7787-0336-3 (RLB)
  1. Wrestling--Juvenile literature. [1. Wrestling.] I. Rouse, Bonna, ill.
II. Crabtree, Marc, ill. III. Title. IV. Series: Sports In Action.
  GV1195.3.C76 2003
  796.812--dc21
                                                                2003001834
Printed in the USA/032010/CG20100208   LC

Contents

What is wrestling?

Wrestling is a physical contest between two athletes. Wrestlers use their muscles as well as their minds to gain control over their opponents. In a wrestling **match**, or contest, two wrestlers try to restrain each other. Each wrestler's goal is to force the other's shoulders to the **mat**. If a wrestler **pins**, or holds, the opponent's shoulders on the mat, he or she wins the match.

While trying to pin the opponent, each wrestler must also try to avoid getting pinned. The wrestlers score points for the moves they use to control their opponents, as well as for moves they use to free themselves from their opponents' grips. In a match with no pin, the wrestler with the most points at the end wins. Turn to page 13 for more on scoring.

Size 'em up

To keep wrestling matches fair, there are different **classes**, or divisions, based on a wrestler's weight, age, and gender. A wrestler competes only against an opponent from the same class.

A long history

Many people associate wrestling with the ancient Greeks and their Olympics, but the sport is much older than that. It dates back at least 15,000 years—long before the time of the ancient Greeks! The sport did become an important part of ancient Greek culture, however, and was the most prestigious Olympic event.

Coming to America

The ancient Romans learned wrestling from the Greeks. The sport spread throughout the Roman Empire, which covered much of Europe. Several centuries later, early settlers brought the sport from Europe to North America, where it became popular at fairs. The first national competition in the United States was held in 1888. The first wrestling event in the modern Olympics was held in 1904. Only men wrestled at the Olympics until 2004, when women's wrestling also became an event.

Early settlers from Europe brought wrestling to North America.

Not the same as pro wrestling

This book is about **amateur wrestling**. You can find amateur wrestling at schools, local gyms, colleges, and international competitions. It is not the same as **professional**, or **pro**, wrestling, which is seen on television and in sports arenas. Although pro wrestlers must be in great physical shape, their performances are not part of an actual sport. They are meant to shock and entertain crowds.

Styles of wrestling

There are three styles of wrestling—**folkstyle**, **freestyle**, and **Greco-Roman**. Folkstyle and freestyle are the styles practiced most often by young wrestlers in North America. The three styles of wrestling are similar, but there are differences between them in scoring, match length, and basic rules. A coach can help you learn more about how to wrestle in the style you choose.

Keep your legs to yourself

Greco-Roman is the oldest style of wrestling. The term "Greco-Roman" is a combination of "Greece" and "Rome." This style is best described as "no legs allowed!" Wrestlers cannot use their legs to hold or trip opponents. They also cannot grab their opponents anywhere below the waist. Wrestlers must try to throw their opponents to the mat or pull them down using only hands and arms. For years, only men wrestled Greco-Roman style, but more women are now wrestling this way.

This wrestler is ready for a Greco-Roman match.

Feel free

Both men and women wrestle freestyle. It is called "freestyle" because its rules are freer than Greco-Roman rules. Freestyle wrestlers are allowed to grip their opponents by the legs and may use their arms as well as their legs to hold opponents.

The American way

Folkstyle wrestling is the most common style for young wrestlers in the United States. It is practiced by students in elementary schools, high schools, and colleges all across the country. As in freestyle wrestling, folkstyle wrestlers are allowed to hold opponents with their legs. They can also grab opponents by the legs. The folkstyle scoring system is slightly different from the freestyle system, however, and certain freestyle moves are not allowed. Folkstyle rules vary slightly from place to place. A coach can tell you more about the folkstyle rules in your area.

*Folkstyle wrestlers are the only wrestlers who must wear **head gear** at all times.*

A freestyle wrestler may hold an opponent's legs.

7

The essentials

Wrestling does not require much equipment. A wrestler's uniform is a sleek one-piece outfit called a **singlet**. The singlet is tight-fitting so that it does not get in the way or give an opponent something to grab.

In fact, grabbing an opponent's uniform is not allowed. Wrestlers can also wear protective equipment such as knee pads. Folkstyle wrestlers must wear head gear, which covers and protects their ears from accidental injury.

Girls' singlets have higher necklines than boys' singlets have.

head gear

folkstyle singlets

knee pad

It is important to have water or a sports beverage with you during a match or practice. Do not drink large amounts at once. Take small sips every ten minutes or so.

Freestyle singlets are cut much lower in the front than folkstyle singlets are.

Wrestling shoes have grooved rubber soles that grip the mat so the wrestler does not slip. The shoes usually cover the ankles for extra support.

The mat

Wrestling matches take place on a round mat. The mat is 28 to 40 feet (8.5 to 12.2 m) across and two to three inches (5-7.5 cm) thick. It is made of foam that is covered by a plastic surface. The mat is marked with two circles. The **inner circle** is about ten feet (3 m) across.

Wrestlers stand inside it at the start of a match. When a wrestler steps outside the larger **outer circle**, he or she is **out-of-bounds**. The match stops, and the wrestlers move back inside the inner circle to start again. For safety reasons, always wrestle on a mat with your coach nearby.

A folkstyle match has at least two officials. A **referee** is on the mat to award points and watch over the match. The **judge** keeps score and assists the referee from the edge of the mat.

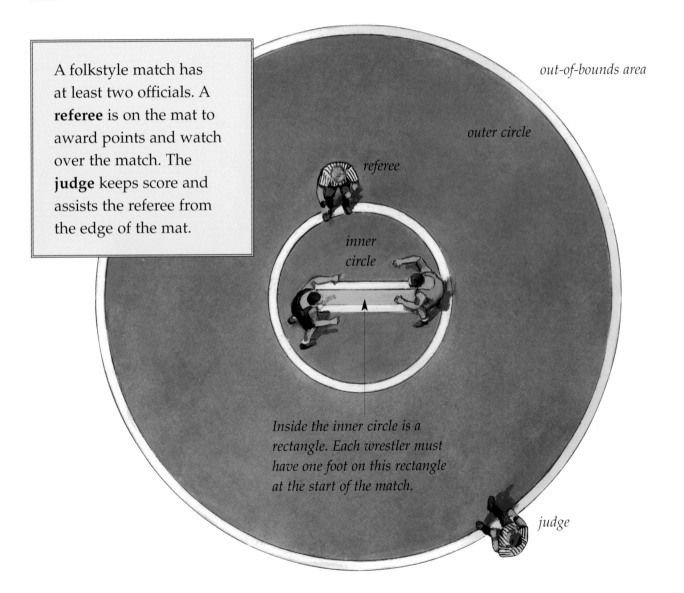

out-of-bounds area

outer circle

referee

inner circle

Inside the inner circle is a rectangle. Each wrestler must have one foot on this rectangle at the start of the match.

judge

Warming up

Wrestling uses just about every muscle in your body. You will twist, turn, push, and pull a lot in the course of a match. You can reduce your chances of injury by warming up before a practice or a match. Warm up for about five minutes with a brisk walk or jog and then do the warm-up exercises shown on these pages. Remember to breathe normally as you move into and hold each of the stretches.

Quadriceps stretch

Lift up your right foot behind you until you can grab it with your right hand. Pull gently until you feel the stretch down the front of your right thigh. Hold the stretch for a count of ten and then switch to stretch your left leg.

Arm circles

Stand with your arms out to your sides at shoulder height. Reach as far as you can with your fingertips so you feel your arms and shoulders stretch. Slowly make small, forward circles with your arms. Make the circles bigger and bigger. When the circles are as big as you can make them, stop and reverse the motion. Do big backward circles and make them smaller and smaller. Repeat.

V stretch

Sit with your legs in a V and flex your feet so your toes are up. Keeping your lower back straight, lean forward until you feel a stretch in the back of your legs and buttocks. Hold the stretch for a count of ten.

Hip stretch

Kneel on your left knee with your right foot flat on the floor. Shift your weight forward until your right knee is directly over your ankle. Place your hands on top of each other on your right thigh, just above your knee. Hold for 10 to 15 seconds. Repeat with your left leg forward.

Building strength

Besides stretches, you should regularly do **strength-building exercises** such as the two shown here. These types of exercises help make your muscles stronger.

Crunches

Lie on your back with your knees bent and your feet flat on the floor. Rest your hands lightly on the back of your head. Press your lower back against the floor and slowly lift your shoulders off the floor. Keep your elbows back. Don't pull your head with your hands! Focus on squeezing your ribs toward your hips and then slowly lower your shoulders to the floor. Do ten crunches.

Pushups

Lie on your front with your hands on the floor beneath your shoulders. Prepare to push up by holding your body rigid from your head to your feet. Straighten your arms to push up and then lower yourself until your nose is about four inches (10 cm) from the mat. Repeat ten times. If you find these pushups too difficult, try pushups with your knees on the floor. Keep your body straight between your head and knees.

Making a match

Folkstyle wrestlers begin each period in different positions, as shown above and below. Before the competitors start wrestling, they must hold their positions and wait until the referee blows the whistle.

The length of a match depends on the wrestling style and age of the competitors. Freestyle and Greco-Roman matches are usually made up of two three-minute periods, with a three-minute overtime when there is a tie. The periods may be shorter for young wrestlers. Most folkstyle matches are made up of three two-minute periods. For younger wrestlers, the periods last one minute each or less.

Starting positions

Freestyle and Greco-Roman matches begin with the wrestlers standing and facing one another in the **neutral position**. In a folkstyle match, each period begins differently. Both wrestlers start the first period in the neutral position (top left). The second period begins with a coin toss. The winner of the toss chooses whether to start in the neutral position or the **referee's position**, in which one wrestler is on top and the other is on the bottom (bottom left). The winner also chooses whether to be in the top or bottom position. The loser of the coin toss makes the same choices at the start of the third period.

Wrestlers must know how to use each starting position to their advantage. Read more about the positions on pages 14 to 15.

Two objectives

After the whistle blows, your first goal is to **gain control**, or be over your opponent. At the same time, you must avoid being controlled by your opponent. You must think and act quickly to achieve both goals!

Attacking and defending

You use **attack** moves, such as **holds** and **throws**, to gain control. Holds are moves in which you grip your opponent with your hands, arms, or legs and try to prevent him or her from moving. Throws are moves that send your opponent quickly to the mat. Throws can lead to scoring a **takedown**. You score a takedown when you get your opponent down on the mat. You use **defensive** moves, such as **escapes** and **reversals**, to keep your opponent from gaining control.

Keep it safe

The object of wrestling is to move, hold, and trap your opponents—not to hurt them! Moves that can injure wrestlers are **illegal**, or not allowed. Any hold that goes against the natural movement of joints is illegal. An example of such a hold is bending your opponent's arm backward.

The top wrestler just scored a takedown and is now in control over her opponent.

Keeping score

Below is a list of the basic points that are awarded in a folkstyle wrestling match. Attack moves and defensive moves both score points. Remember, if at any point in the match you pin your opponent, you win the match!

Takedown (2 points): Getting your opponent down on the mat and gaining control
Nearfall (2 points): Keeping your opponent's shoulders at less than a 45° angle to the mat for at least two seconds. If your nearfall lasts five seconds, you get three points.
Fall (wins the match): Pinning the back of your opponent's shoulders to the mat for two seconds
Escape (1 point): Moving out from under your opponent and getting into a standing position
Reversal (2 points): Moving out from under your opponent and then into a controlling position over your opponent

Take your position

Every match begins with the neutral position. The body pose a wrestler uses in this position is called a **stance**. There are two stances a wrestler can use in the neutral position—the **squared stance** and the **staggered stance**. Try both of them often, so you learn which one feels most comfortable for you and which works best against certain opponents. Whether you use the squared or the staggered stance, one foot must be on the rectangle at the center of the mat.

staggered stance

leading foot

squared stance

The squared stance

Stand with your knees slightly bent and shoulder-width apart. Have your feet just past your knees and point your toes outward. Lean forward at the waist and keep your back straight. Keep your head up and focus on your opponent. Bend your arms at the elbows. Have your hands open and ready to start **grappling**.

The staggered stance

You can spring forward quickly from this aggressive stance. It is almost the same as the squared stance, except one foot—the **leading foot**—is slightly ahead of the other. The leading foot points straight ahead, and the other foot points outward. Your shoulders face forward and your head is up so you can watch your opponent.

The referee's position

Folkstyle wrestlers often use the referee's position to begin the second and third periods. This position is also used to restart play in folkstyle matches after a wrestler goes out-of-bounds. To learn more about how to wrestle from the top and bottom positions, see pages 28 to 31.

The top position

Kneel on your left knee behind your opponent. Your knee should be near his or her left knee. Put your right foot behind your opponent's feet. Place your right hand on your opponent's stomach, over the belly button. Lean forward and look up.

The bottom photo on page 12 shows one version of the referee's position. The one on this page is more common.

The bottom position

Kneel with your knees shoulder-width apart on the mat's center rectangle. Put your palms on the mat and raise your head. Your arms should be in line with your knees. Keep more of your weight on your hips and legs than on your palms.

Tie it up

When starting from a neutral position, neither you nor your opponent has an advantage. You must attack your opponent to get into a better position. Using **tie-ups** is a good way to force your opponent into a weak position. Tie-ups are holds that use one or both hands. They give you a solid grip on your opponent. These holds do not give you full control, however. Instead, they allow you to move your opponent into a position from which you can gain full control. There are many types of tie-ups. Each one can be the first step in scoring a takedown.

*For the **collar tie-up**, put one hand behind your opponent's neck and shove your forearm against his or her chest, as the girl on the right is doing. Keep your other hand firmly locked around your opponent's elbow.*

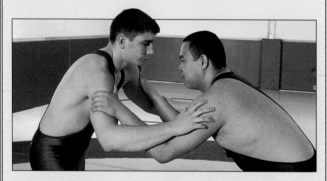

*A **double-inside tie-up** is an easy move to perform. Slip your hands quickly between your opponent's arms and grab the inside of the upper arms. Keep your head up, as the boy on the right is doing.*

Watchful eyes

Using tie-ups requires quick hands and watchful eyes. Keep your head up and watch your opponent. Ask yourself which body part seems easiest to grab. You can apply tie-ups to your opponent's neck, upper arms, wrists, and elbows. The basic tie-ups on the left are some common ways to get a grip on your opponent.

*For a **double-wrist tie-up**, quickly slide your hands down your opponent's arms and firmly grab the wrists, as the girl on the left is doing.*

One-sided

Some tie-ups target one side of your opponent's body. These tie-ups include the **underhook** and the **two-on-one**, which are shown below. Using one of these tie-ups gives you a better chance of pushing your opponent to the side and making him or her unbalanced—which can lead to a takedown. Practice different tie-ups often to discover what each one can do for you in a match.

Keeping your hands in constant motion makes it difficult for your opponent to grab them. It also keeps your opponent guessing about what you will do next.

Underhooks are strong tie-ups. As you grapple, pull down quickly on one of your opponent's arms. With your other arm, sweep under your opponent's free arm and grip the back of his or her shoulder. Push your head against the shoulder.

For the two-on-one, grab one of your opponent's arms with both hands. You can grab the wrist with both hands or use one hand to grab your opponent's wrist and the other hand to grip his or her upper arm, as shown above.

Taking it further

An attack from the side is much more difficult to stop than an attack from the front. Any move that lets you get at your opponent's side is called a **setup**. Setups can help you unbalance your opponent and score takedowns. For most setups, you turn your opponent in one direction while moving around him or her in the other direction.

A setup can be a very simple move such as **passing the arm**, as shown below by the wrestler in blue. As you and your opponent lean in to grapple, grab one of your opponent's elbows or wrists and quickly tug it across your body. This jerking motion briefly unbalances your opponent. Now you can move around quickly to your opponent's side.

When passing the arm, you must act quickly. Your opponent will be unbalanced only for a moment.

Using the tie-up

You can use a tie-up to get a good setup. The tie-up makes the setup easier since you already have a grip on your opponent. With your opponent in a tie-up, you can quickly turn him or her to the side and get ready to score a takedown. This page shows some ways you can use tie-ups to get at your opponent's side.

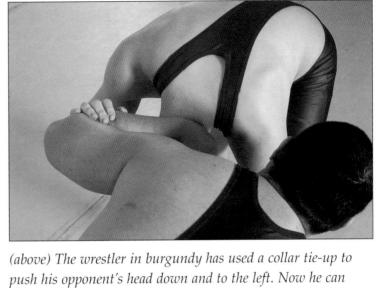

(above) The wrestler in burgundy has used a collar tie-up to push his opponent's head down and to the left. Now he can quickly move to the right to attack his opponent from the side.

Putting your opponent in a two-on-one tie-up puts you in a good position to use a setup.

*The **headlock** is a strong hold that you can apply after a setup. It is very difficult for an opponent to escape from a headlock. The wrestler on the right is now in position to move his opponent to the mat and score a takedown.*

Untying the knot

All wrestlers eventually find themselves caught in a tie-up, so be prepared! Being held in a good tie-up doesn't have to mean you are headed for the mat. You can fight against a tie-up by keeping your balance, attacking the hold, and above all, using your head.

Don't be fooled!

It's best to avoid the trouble caused by tie-ups by staying out of them in the first place. Your opponent may use sudden arm or leg movements to try to fool you into heading in a certain direction. He or she can then lunge at your exposed side and get you in a tie-up. Watch your opponent's body—it will let you know where your opponent is really moving. When grappling, remember to keep your shoulders facing toward your opponent and defend yourself with your arms. Look for areas to attack with your own tie-up.

The wrestler on the left is caught in a tie-up. She pushes on the side of her opponent's head to unbalance and distract her.

Stay balanced

When you are caught in a tie-up, keep your head up and your feet underneath you. Have your feet a little more than shoulder-width apart and your knees bent to maintain your balance. Take short, quick steps to keep your feet under you as your opponent pulls and pushes. You can better attack the tie-up when you are balanced.

The tied-up wrestler on the right stays balanced by keeping her knees bent and her feet apart.

The weakest link

To free yourself from an opponent's grip, think of his or her hand as a giant sticker you have to peel off. Work your fingers underneath the pinky-finger side of your opponent's hand, where the grip is weaker. The pinky is easier to get under and pry up than the thumb and forefinger are.

Where are you taking me?

Whenever you're in a tie-up, your opponent will try to move you in a certain direction. For example, from a collar tie-up, your opponent may try to lower you into a headlock. Learn to ask yourself, "Where is my opponent trying to move me?" and then stop that from happening. You may not always guess correctly, but you will learn to think constantly while you are on the mat.

When your arm is caught in a tie-up, peel away your opponent's hand starting with the pinky.

If you cannot reach your opponent's hand, grab the wrist instead to remove the grip.

21

Takedowns!

Takedowns help you score points. They also place your opponent in a position to be pinned. Before you can perform a takedown, you need to get **inside**, or right up against, your opponent. The **penetration step** is often the first move you'll use to score takedowns.

The penetration step can be done right from the neutral position. This move gets you close enough to grab your opponent around the waist. Although you must lower your shoulders, don't drop your head. Keep your head up and focus on your opponent.

For the penetration step, bend low at the hips and take a big step forward so you're under your opponent's arms. Reach out with one arm and grab your opponent around the waist. Pull your opponent toward you and wrap both arms around the hips.

The penetration step

Be sure to make your penetration step quick and forceful. Push hard against your opponent's waist.

After the penetration step, grab the back of your opponent's thighs. Drive your shoulder into your opponent's stomach area and push up with your legs. Next, tilt downward and slam your opponent to the mat.

Double trouble

The **double-leg takedown** is one of the most powerful moves in wrestling. It is the first takedown most wrestlers learn. It is so effective that they continue to use it even at higher levels of competition.

Use the power of your legs to explode forward and drive your opponent down to the mat.

outside single-leg takedown

single-leg takedown

*The **single-leg takedown** and the **outside single-leg takedown** are two basic takedowns. After the penetration step, grab one of your opponent's legs and lift it off the ground. Twist your opponent down to the mat. The outside single-leg takedown often starts from a kneeling position. The single-leg takedown allows you to trap your opponent's leg between your arms and legs.*

Finish the job

After you make a solid takedown, your opponent will be stunned briefly and trapped under your weight. You have the advantage, but don't relax! Attack quickly before your opponent has a chance to recover from the takedown. If you're slow to move in to pin your opponent, the referee can call you for **stalling** and award points to your opponent! Stalling is called when you're in control, but don't try to pin your opponent.

Use your body weight as part of a finishing hold. After a takedown, this wrestler acted quickly to stay on top of her opponent. Her weight is firmly on her opponent's shoulders and chest.

The last word

A **finishing hold** is one way to keep up the pressure on your opponent. There are many types of finishing holds. A coach can teach you which one works best with each takedown. Remember that, with the finishing hold, you're trying to trap your opponent's shoulders for a pin.

The wrestler in burgundy is in control but if he holds this position for too long, the referee will call him for stalling. By driving forward with his shoulders and legs, he can get his opponent flat on the mat.

From start to finish

It's one thing to understand how to do the many wrestling moves and holds, but in a match, you must also know the best ways to combine them to attack and escape from your opponent. The pictures below show one possible combination of moves that can be used from a neutral position. The wrestler with the blue head gear goes from grappling, to using a tie-up, to scoring a takedown, to applying a finishing hold, and finally, to making a pin.

As the wrestlers grapple, the one in blue head gear puts a double-inside tie-up on his opponent's shoulders.

He slips one hand on his opponent's upper arm. He puts his other hand on the wrist for a two-on-one tie-up.

He drags the arm down. He then takes a penetration step to move in and start a single-leg takedown.

The wrestler quickly lifts up his opponent and then drives him down to the mat. He scores two points!

He traps his opponent's leg between his legs and leans forward. His weight keeps his opponent down.

He hooks his opponent's leg and pushes his shoulders down to the mat. He holds the move for a pin!

25

Countermoves

When your opponent moves toward you for a takedown, you must act quickly to stop the attack. There are several **countermoves** that help you keep your balance and avoid an attack. They not only stop your opponent but can also lead to a takedown of your own! In fact, many countermoves involve using an opponent's attack against him or her. In the photo above, the wrestler in burgundy is attacking with a penetration step. To make this attack, she must have her head down low. The wrestler in red uses this opportunity to turn things around. She holds her opponent's head in this position to gain control, even though her opponent started the attack.

Lean into the attack

Normally, you want to keep your shoulders above your hips for balance. During a takedown attack, however, your opponent is pushing into you. If you stand up straight, you'll fall backward. Instead, lean hard into your opponent. Refuse to be pushed back! Keep your legs apart and dig your toes into the mat. The **sprawl** (below) is an example of this type of countermove.

Tumbling down

As you lean into your opponent's attack, one of you may slip. Both of you may then tumble out of control. When you find yourself falling, do your best to stay facing your opponent. Try to stand up quickly and back away from him or her. If you land on top of your opponent, stay where you are and work hard to keep him or her down on the mat.

1. As your opponent drives against you, lean your hip forward and push down on your opponent's shoulder and head.

2. Slide your feet backward and push one hand down on the back of your opponent's neck. Stay on your toes as you drive your opponent down to the mat.

①

*To perform an **elbow-hip breakdown**, reach under your opponent's arm with one hand and slide the other around to your opponent's other hip or inner thigh. Pull both your arms outward, taking your opponent's arm and leg with them. Your opponent cannot help but fall to the mat.*

②

A half-nelson is a hold in which you hook one arm under your opponent's arm and across the back of the neck. Your other arm is free to restrain your opponent further.

Higher power

When you start in the top position, half your work is done for you—your opponent is already on the mat and underneath you. You're not finished yet, though! You need to know how to stay in control and move quickly to a pin.

Breakdowns

Although your opponent is down on the mat, he or she is in a stable position. **Breakdowns** are moves that get your opponent off his or her hands and knees and flat on the mat. These moves stretch out your opponent's arms and legs so that he or she cannot support your weight and must collapse on the mat.

Turn over

After a breakdown, your opponent is facedown on the mat and unable to attack. Now you can work to get the pin and win the match. A hold such as a **half-nelson**, shown left, allows you to turn your opponent over onto his or her back. The hold restrains your opponent's arms so that he or she cannot escape.

Rock-a-bye

A **cradle** is another type of move that helps you turn over an opponent after a breakdown. There are many types of cradles, but all of them involve grabbing your opponent's head with one hand and a leg with your other hand. You then squeeze your arms together and flip your opponent's body.

Reach across the back of your opponent's head to grab the opposite shoulder. Press against the back with your shoulder or chest.

Slide your other hand to the inside of your opponent's knee. Bring your arms together until they meet and then lean back.

Pull your opponent's legs up and backward until they are high in the air. Your opponent's shoulders are now pinned on the mat.

Get under it

When you start in the bottom position, you must fight to stay up as soon as the whistle blows. Your opponent will be trying to stretch out your limbs and get you flat on your chest. To score an escape, you have to get back on your feet. Getting to your feet helps you score reversals, too. Start by trying to get your hips underneath your shoulders and then straighten your back to stay balanced. Push back hard against your opponent and try to stand up one leg at a time.

When in the bottom position, remember to push back against your opponent. Keep your weight mostly over your knees and hips, not your hands.

Put a spin on it

Spinning out is a great way to score a reversal. As your opponent reaches to apply a hold, you scoot out from under him or her and swing around to the top position! Now you're ready to try a breakdown.

Make your spin smooth and quick. Try to surprise your opponent.

Don't stop struggling

The key to wrestling in the bottom position is to struggle as much as possible and break your opponent's grip. As you work to break the grip, think of ways you can turn the move into an attack of your own. For example, by holding on to your opponent's arm, you can flip him or her over your body. Doing so breaks the grip and puts your opponent on the mat, ready for you to take control. In general, try to keep your chest toward the mat—your opponent cannot pin you unless you are on your back.

If your opponent reaches for an ankle, break the grip by grabbing the wrist and lifting your leg away.

1. Standing up is a simple way to score an escape from the bottom position. Grab your opponent's hands and hold them at the wrists. Lean back hard.

2. Work at getting up one foot at a time. Keep pressure on your opponent's chest until you are fully on your feet. When you're up, turn quickly to face your opponent.

Glossary

Note: Boldfaced words that are defined in the book may not appear in the glossary.

attack Any move that lets you gain control of your opponent

breakdown A move that pushes your opponent off the hands and knees to a flat position

countermove A move made in response to an opponent's move in order to avoid an attack

defensive Describing a move that protects a wrestler from attack

escape A move that brings you out from under an opponent to a standing position

finishing hold A hold intended to pin your opponent's shoulders to the mat

grapple To grip an opponent tightly

hold A move in which you grip an opponent with hands, arms, or legs

mat A padded layer that covers the floor

neutral position A starting position with the legs bent and the arms bent close to the body

penetration step A move that brings you close to your opponent

pin To hold an opponent's shoulders to the floor

referee's position A starting position with one wrestler on top and the other on the bottom

reversal A move that brings a wrestler out from under an opponent to a position of control

setup A move that allows a wrestler to attack an opponent from the side

takedown A move that forces an opponent down on the mat

tie-up A hold that uses one or both hands to grip an opponent

Index